WELCOME TO MY COUNTRY

Welcome to
JORDAN

Gareth Stevens Publishing
A WORLD ALMANAC EDUCATION GROUP COMPANY

Written by
GRACE PUNDYK

Edited by
MELVIN NEO

Edited in USA by
JENETTE DONOVAN GUNTLY

Designed by
GEOSLYN LIM

Picture research by
SUSAN JANE MANUEL

First published in North America in 2005 by
Gareth Stevens Publishing
A World Almanac Education Group Company
330 West Olive Street, Suite 100
Milwaukee, Wisconsin 53212 USA

Please visit our web site at
www.garethstevens.com
For a free color catalog describing
Gareth Stevens Publishing's list of high-quality
books and multimedia programs,
call 1-800-542-2595 (USA) or
1-800-387-3178 (Canada).
Gareth Stevens Publishing's fax: (414) 332-3567.

© **MARSHALL CAVENDISH INTERNATIONAL (ASIA)
PRIVATE LIMITED 2004**
Originated and designed by
Times Editions Marshall Cavendish
An imprint of Marshall Cavendish International (Asia) Pte Ltd
A member of Times Publishing Limited
Times Centre, 1 New Industrial Road
Singapore 536196
http://www.timesone.com.sg/te

Library of Congress Cataloging-in-Publication Data
Pundyk, Grace.
Welcome to Jordan / by Grace Pundyk.
p. cm. — (Welcome to my country)
Includes bibliographical references and index.
ISBN 0-8368-2565-9 (lib. bdg.)
1. Jordan — Juvenile literature. [1. Jordan.] I. Title. II. Series.
DS153.P86   2004
956.95—dc22   2003070404

Printed in Singapore

1 2 3 4 5 6 7 8 9 08 07 06 05 04

PICTURE CREDITS
Agence France Presse: 29, 33, 36 (bottom)
A.N.A. Press Agency: 27 (bottom), 31
Art Directors and TRIP Photo Library:
    5, 17, 21, 25 (top), 26, 43
Bes Stock: 2
Michele Burgess: 11, 32
Focus Team — Italy: 4, 6, 15 (bottom),
    20, 22, 40
Getty Images/HultonArchive: 12, 13,
    14, 15 (top), 16, 23, 39
Michel Gunther/Still Pictures: 3 (bottom)
Haga Library, Japan: cover, 28 (bottom)
Sonia Halliday Photographs: 1, 24
Israelimages.com: 38
Klein/Hubert/Still Pictures: 3 (center), 45
Lonely Planet Images: 7, 9, 19, 28 (top),
    34, 36 (top), 37
North Wind Picture Archives: 10
Christine Osborne Pictures: 3 (top), 8, 18,
    25 (bottom), 27 (top), 30 (top), 35, 41
Travel Ink: 30 (bottom)

Digital Scanning by Superskill Graphics Pte Ltd

Contents

Words that appear in the glossary are printed in **boldface** type the first time they occur in the text.

Welcome to Jordan!

The Hashemite Kingdom of Jordan is located in southwest Asia. The country is part of an ancient region known as Palestine. Jordan's rich culture comes from its long history and the many **ethnic** groups that have lived in the country. Let's visit Jordan and learn about its interesting people!

Opposite: The people of Jordan are proud of their former ruler, King Hussein. Pictures of him still hang in shops and homes all over Jordan.

Below: In summer, both Jordanians and tourists attend the Jerash Festival of Culture and Arts.

The Flag of Jordan

The black, white, and green stripes on Jordan's flag stand for the Abbasid, Umayyad, and Fatimid **dynasties**. The red triangle represents the Hashemite dynasty. The seven-pointed star symbolizes the first seven verses of the Koran, the holy book of Islam.

The Land

Jordan has an area of 35,637 square miles (92,300 square kilometers). The country is almost completely **encircled** by land. Jordan's only coastline borders the Gulf of Aqaba, which is located to the southwest. The country's coast is only 16 miles (26 kilometers) long.

A desert called the Syrian, or North Arabian, Desert covers most of eastern and southern Jordan. The land in the desert, and in other areas of Jordan, is so dry that almost nothing can grow.

Below:
These beautiful rock formations and pink desert sand are unique to Wadi Rum in southern Jordan.

Jabal Ram is Jordan's highest point at 5,689 feet (1,734 meters). It is in the country's uplands, an area of high **elevation** in the north. Jordan's best farmland is found in the west, in the Jordan Valley. In the center of the valley is the Dead Sea, the lowest body of water on Earth. It lies 1,312 feet (400 m) below sea level and contains so many **minerals** and so much salt that no plants or animals can live in it.

Climate

The climate of western Jordan is mild all year because that region is nearest to the Mediterranean Sea. In the east and south of Jordan, the desert climate is hot in summer and cold in winter. In Amman, Jordan's capital city, summer temperatures can reach 79° Fahrenheit (26° Celsius). Winter temperatures can fall to 46° F (8° C). Jordan only gets a little rain during its short winter season.

Above: Snow often falls during winter in the city of Irbid in northern Jordan.

Plants and Animals

In northwest Jordan, trees such as oak, pistachio, and eucalyptus grow. Acacia trees, shrubs, and grasses grow in the deserts. Too much hunting and the growth of cities reduced the numbers of plants and animals in the country, so Jordan created many nature **reserves**. The reserves help protect animals such as the Arabian oryx, the Nubian ibex, goitered gazelles, and Persian onagers. About 150 kinds of birds live in Jordan, including griffon vultures.

Left: Many rare kinds of marine life, including several types of coral, live in the waters of the Gulf of Aqaba. The city of Aqaba serves as the country's only port, and it is also a tourist spot. Large numbers of ships and people have damaged the gulf's marine life. Jordanian officials have set up an area of the gulf that will be left untouched.

History

The land that is now Jordan was the site of some of the world's earliest human settlements, dating from the Stone Age.

Jordan long has been an important location along the Arabian trade route, which merchants traveled to sell goods. By the 1200s B.C., kingdoms had been established in the area. The Israelites ruled Jordan in about 1000 B.C. Later, the Assyrians, the Babylonians, and the Persians ruled Jordan. In 332 B.C., Alexander the Great took control.

Left: The kingdom of Edom, as shown in this illustration, was established by the 1200s B.C. Edom was located in the southern region of what is now Jordan. It was built around the Arabian trade route, which helped Edom grow wealthy. Other kingdoms were formed at about the same time, including Ammon in the north and Moab in the central region.

Left: This Christian castle near Shobak was built in 1115. It served as a fortress during the time of the Crusades, which were wars fought by Christians of the Byzantine Empire against Muslims. In 1189, the castle was overrun by the Muslim army.

After Alexander's death, several smaller kingdoms ruled the Jordan area until the Romans **conquered** Jordan in 63 B.C. The Romans helped trade grow and built grand buildings. In A.D. 636, Arabs invaded northern Jordan. They were Muslims, or people who followed the Islamic religion, and they brought their beliefs to Jordan. A series of Arab dynasties, including the Umayyads and the Abbasids, ruled the region until 1517, when the Ottoman Turks took control. Jordan was part of the Ottoman **Empire** for the next four centuries.

From the Ottomans to Transjordan

The Ottomans did not take good care of Jordan's economy or public works. Resentment grew among the country's residents. In 1916, the king of Hejaz, Husayn ibn 'Ali, and his sons, Abdullah and Faysal, led a **revolt** against the Ottomans. The British helped the king and took control of the region after World War I. The new British Mandate of Palestine was broken into two parts. The land west of the Jordan River was named Palestine. The land to the east became Transjordan.

A Nation Is Born

On March 22, 1946, Transjordan became independent. On March 25, Abdullah named himself king. In 1949, the country's name was changed to the Hashemite Kingdom of Jordan. From 1948 to 1982, Jordan and other Arab nations fought several wars against Israel. In 1951, after Jordan **annexed** a part of Palestine, Palestinian Arabs killed King Abdullah. In 1953, his grandson Hussein became king.

Below: Young King Hussein spoke to soldiers at a military camp in Jordan on August 11, 1958. Hussein was just eighteen years old when he became king of Jordan.

A Peaceful Jordan

Fighting between Israel and Jordan's Arab neighbors continued. Palestinians living in Jordan began to secretly fight the Israelis, too. King Hussein made the Palestinians leave. Jordan fought another war with Israel in 1973, and in 1977, all ties between the two nations were cut. By 1994, however, the two nations had signed a peace agreement. Under King Hussein's rule, Jordan became one of the most **stable** and peaceful nations in the Middle East.

Left: After King Hussein died in 1999, his son, Abdullah II (*left*), became king. Abdullah met with Ehud Barak, the Israeli prime minister, in Israel on April 23, 2000.

King Abdullah I (1882–1951)

In 1916, Abdullah, son of the king of Hejaz, helped lead a revolt against the Ottomans. In 1921, he was made emir. He later became the first king of independent Jordan. In 1951, he was killed by Palestinian Arabs.

King Abdullah I

Queen Zein (1916–1994)

King Hussein's mother, Queen Zein, played a key role in Jordan's politics and also strongly supported women's rights. In 1944, she started Jordan's first women's union. She helped write the 1952 Constitution, which gave women full rights.

King Hussein (1935–1999)

A respected leader, King Hussein ruled Jordan for forty-five years. He helped strengthen the economy and improved daily living conditions. One of his greatest successes was his historic peace agreement with Israel.

King Hussein

Government and the Economy

Jordan is a **constitutional monarchy** with legislative, executive, and judicial branches of government. The country's National Assembly has two parts: the Senate and the House of Deputies. The king chooses members of the Senate, and voters elect members of the House of Deputies. The king also chooses a prime minister, who then selects the members of the Council of Ministers.

Below: In 2000, King Abdullah II (*front row, sixth from left*), posed on the steps of the Raghadan Royal Palace in Amman with his ministers. The king has a lot of power in Jordan. He can fire the Council of Ministers or break up the National Assembly without anyone else's permission.

Jordan has three types of courts: civil, religious, and special. The civil courts deal with citizens' lawsuits and criminal issues. Jordan's Muslim and non-Muslim religious courts oversee **inheritance**, marriage, divorce, and child custody cases. The special courts deal with military or national security cases. All of the courts are overseen by the Higher Judicial Council.

For its local government, Jordan is divided into twelve **governorates** and smaller districts and subdistricts.

The Economy

Jordan's economy has grown in recent years, but about 30 percent of its people are very poor. Farming was once the country's main source of income. In 1967, Israel took control of the land Jordan had annexed in Palestine. The loss of the land hurt the economy because it was some of Jordan's best farmland. Today, only 3 percent of Jordan's land is farmed, and very few Jordanians are farmers.

Above:
These women are tending fields in the Jordan Valley, which today holds almost all of the country's farms. Cucumbers, citrus fruits, and melons are just a few of the crops grown in the Jordan Valley.

Jordan has large deposits of minerals such as limestone, marble, and salt. It also has large deposits of **phosphates**. The mining of phosphates is Jordan's biggest industry, and the mineral is also the country's main **export**. Jordan's other exports include manufactured goods, fertilizers, and farming products.

Jordan does not have any deposits of oil, however. The country must buy all the oil it needs for fuel and energy from Iraq, Jordan's neighbor. Other **imports** include animals, food, and machinery. The country relies on tourism and other industries to bring money into Jordan.

Left: Tourism to sites like Petra, one of the seven ancient wonders of the world, helps Jordan's economy.

People and Lifestyle

About 98 percent of the people of Jordan are Arab. They can be divided into three groups: the Transjordanians, the Palestinian Arabs, and the Bedouin. Transjordanians live east of the Jordan River. They settled in the area before 1948. Palestinian Arabs either are refugees from war or came from the West Bank. The Bedouin are often regarded as the area's native people.

Below: In the Jordan Valley, a young Jordanian boy poses next to his colorfully decorated horse.

Left:
Mount Nebo, where these children are playing, is located in the governorate of Madaba. Mount Nebo and Madaba are famous for their ancient **mosaics**.

The Bedouin have lived in the Jordan area for centuries and have most often been **nomadic**. They live mainly in Jordan's desert regions. Today, many Bedouin have chosen to settle in towns and villages across the country. They play important roles in Jordan's army and political, economic, and social life and are very loyal to the royal family.

Other groups, such as the Circassians, Armenians, and Chechens, make up only 2 percent of Jordan's population.

Family Life

Families are at the center of life in Jordan. Often, many family members live in the same area. Jordanian fathers are usually the decision makers, and mothers are expected to stay home and care for the children. The birth of a child is a joyous event in Jordan, and children are treasured by society. The parents often make many **sacrifices** for their children's care and education.

City and Country Living

About 75 percent of the Jordanian people live in apartments or houses in the cities. The buildings are made of stone and cement, and almost all of them have electricity and access to water. In the country, Jordanians live in villages. Their homes are built of stone and mud or concrete. Some of these homes have no electricity or water.

Almost two million **refugees** from Palestine live in Jordan. Many of them live in crowded refugee camps outside Jordan's major cities. Life is very hard for the people living in these camps.

Left: In Jordan, getting married is often the most important, and the most expensive, event in a person's life. Many Jordanian couples are now getting married in mass weddings so that the costs can be shared.

Education

Jordan's school system has improved a lot in recent decades. Today, education is available to all Jordanians, and about 87 percent of Jordanians can read and write. Most children go to free schools run by the government, and the country also has several private schools. From the ages of six to fifteen, children must attend school, but they may stop after tenth grade. Jordanian children study subjects such as biology, the Arabic language, mathematics, and English.

Below:
These students are lining up to go to class at a school in Amman. Jordan's government makes sure that even in very small or poor towns, all children can go to school.

After tenth grade, Jordanian students enter secondary school. They can choose between an academic and a **vocational** program. Academic students can go on to a university if they pass the *Tawjihi* (tow-JEE-hee), the general secondary exam, after two years. Vocational program students work as **apprentices** and learn to be skilled laborers. After the two-year program, these students can go to a community college and study subjects such as education, computers, or nursing.

Above: Philadelphia University is near Amman. Jordan's first university was the University of Jordan, which was founded in 1962.

Below: This teacher at a school in Amman is checking a student's work.

Religion

Jordan's official religion is Islam. Its followers are called Muslims. Islam is divided into two branches: the Sunni and the Shi'ite. In Jordan, 92 percent of Muslims are Sunnis. Muslims must live by the Five Pillars of Islam, a set of rules. Muslims must declare their faith by reciting a statement about God and Muhammad, pray five times a day, donate money to the poor, fast during the holy month of Ramadan, and make a **pilgrimage** to the holy city of Mecca.

Above: The King Abdullah Mosque, in northwestern Amman, was built in honor of King Abdullah I by his grandson, King Hussein. The mosque is also called the Blue Dome Mosque.

There are mosques, or Muslim houses of worship, all over Jordan. Men pray in the front of the mosque, and women pray at the back, either at floor level or on a **mezzanine**. After Friday prayers, many Muslims stay at the mosque to meet with relatives and friends and to exchange news.

Non-Muslim religions are present in Jordan as well. About 6 percent of all Jordanians are Christian, and most of them go to Greek Orthodox churches.

Below: This old Christian Bible, which is written in Arabic, is displayed in a church in the city of Madaba. There are Christian churches in several areas of Jordan.

Language

Arabic is Jordan's official language. It is an ancient language, and different versions are spoken throughout the Arab world. Many ethnic groups speak Arabic in addition to their own languages. Arabic is written and read from right to left. The twenty-eight letters are based on eighteen different shapes. Marks added above or below eight of the shapes form more letters.

Many Jordanians also speak English, which is taught in Jordan's schools.

Above: In Jordan, most newspapers and magazines are in Arabic. Only one of its newspapers is in English, the *Jordan Times*.

Left: Most of the road signs in Jordan are written in both Arabic and English.

Literature

Jordan's literature began to develop in the twentieth century. Today, Jordan's writers and poets are regarded as some of the best in the Arab world. Honor, love, war, and political change are just a few of the subjects they write about. Mustafa Wahbi at-Tal (1899–1949) is Jordan's best-known poet. Mahmoud Sayf ad-Din al-Irani (1914–1974) was an early writer of short stories in Arabic. Women writers include Fadwa Tuqan (1917–), Samira Azzam (1927–1967), and Diana Abu-Jaber (1959–).

Arts

The arts are important in Jordan and reflect the country's long history as well as its rich culture and tradition.

Architecture

Jordan is home to many architectural treasures. The ancient cities of Petra and Jerash, Madaba's colorful mosaics, and the magnificent mosques built by Muslim Jordanians are all reminders of the country's unique **heritage**.

Above: This man is using tiny funnels to create colorful patterns in sand. Making bottled sand is a popular craft in Jordan.

Left: Bottled sand can be made into many designs, including circles, squares, triangles, plants, animals, and scenes from the desert. The sand is packed down to stop the design from moving around.

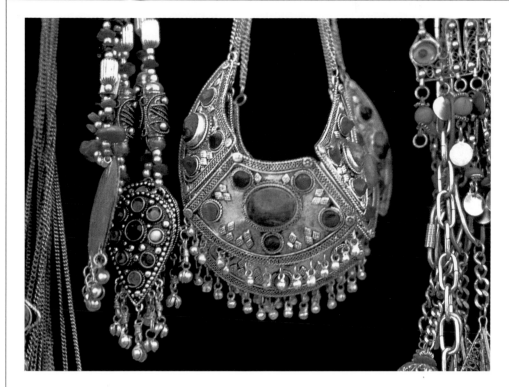

Traditional Crafts

Many of Jordan's traditional crafts are used in everyday life, but they often are made with beautiful decorations. Quilts and clothes often have colorful sewing on them. Some picture frames may be covered in mother-of-pearl, which is the pearly lining of a type of seashell. Brass and copper are beaten to make coffee pots and household items. The Bedouin are famous for woven rugs, which are made of sheep's or camel's wool and come in many patterns.

Music

Jordanians enjoy many types of music and often play traditional instruments in their modern songs. Some traditional instruments include the *oud* (OOD), which is a wooden lute, and the *dhuff*, which is shaped like a tambourine. Others are the *nay*, which is a reed flute used to play classical music, and the many-stringed *qanun* (KAH-noon).

Above:
Omar Elat is a well-known Jordanian musician. This picture shows him performing at Amman's Royal Cultural Center on June 1, 2002.

Dances

Jordan has many local and regional dances. One popular dance is the lively *debka*, which women and men dance separately. Dancers stomp their feet and clap their hands to the sounds of a single drum. In the *sahjeh*, a well-known Bedouin dance, dancers act out stories of heroes from the past.

Theater

Jordanian plays first became known in the early twentieth century. Many of the plays tell stories about the people or events that have changed the region.

Opposite:
This Jordanian man is playing a traditional string instrument as he sits outside the ancient city of Petra.

Leisure

Because most Jordanians do not have a lot of money, much of their leisure time is spent with family and friends. Social occasions, such as weddings, are major forms of entertainment. Dancing and singing are often part of the fun. Going on picnics is another favorite pastime.

In the cities, many young Jordanians enjoy dining out with friends and going to the movies. Wealthier city dwellers enjoy theater performances as well.

Below: Jordanians love going to the movies. This hand-painted poster is advertising a film showing at a movie theater in Amman.

Jordanian men go to coffeehouses, where they drink coffee, talk, and listen to music. They also like to play board games in their free time. Popular games are backgammon, chess, and *shutterunge* (shu-terr-UNJ), a game similar to chess and checkers. Children in Jordan love playing outdoor games. Some of these games, such as *hajli* (HAJ-lee), a type of hopscotch, have been handed down from generation to generation. Many Jordanian boys like to play *ghalool* (GHA-lool), or marbles.

Above: In summer, many Jordanian families enjoy visiting the beaches located around the seaport of Aqaba.

Sports

Jordanians enjoy playing many sports. Soccer is by far the most popular sport in Jordan, and it is played at the local, regional, and national levels. Two of the country's favorite soccer teams are Al-Wehdat and Al-Faisaly.

Above: Because King Abdullah II is a big soccer fan, many stadiums in Jordan display pictures of him dressed in the national soccer team's colors.

Horse racing and horse jumping are also popular in Jordan. The country has many world-class athletes in horseback-riding events. Princess Haya Bint Al Hussein represented Jordan at the 2000 Olympic Games.

Left: Wadi Rum, in the south of Jordan, is one of the most challenging rock-climbing locations in the world.

Jordan has many excellent athletes in gymnastics and the martial arts. In 2001, Jordan won first place in the Amman International Gymnastics Championship. That same year, the country's men's and women's karate teams won first and second place in the Middle East Championships.

Car rallying, a type of car racing, is another favorite sport in Jordan. The famous Jordan International Car Rally is a long-distance desert race.

Opposite: This group of jockeys is taking part in a horse-racing event held in Amman.

Religious Festivals

Many of Jordan's festivals are religious. During Ramadan, the Islamic holy month, Muslims do not eat, drink, or smoke until sunset each day. *Eid al-Fitr* (EED al-FIH-tur) is a three-day festival at the end of Ramadan. *Eid al-Adha* (EED al-AD-ah) honors Abraham's willingness to kill his son on God's orders. The festival follows the *hajj* (HAJ), or Islamic pilgrimage to Mecca.

Below: These Jordanian Muslims are praying at a mosque during the Islamic holy month of Ramadan.

National Holidays and Festivals

Jordan's national holidays and festivals generally mark important events in the country's recent history, remember the nation's kings, or celebrate the arts. In the summer each year, Jordan holds the Jerash Festival, which is a famous arts festival. Artists from around the world come to act in plays, perform dances, read poetry, play music, and exhibit art and crafts. The festival can be traced back to Roman times. It has become Jordan's main showcase for its cultural and performing arts.

Food

Cooking in Jordan has been influenced by the Bedouins and by the foods of neighboring countries, such as Syria and Lebanon. Lamb, chicken, grains, cheese, vegetables, and fresh and dried fruit are often used in Jordan's dishes. The use of yogurt, herbs, spices, and nuts gives Jordanian cooking much of its unique flavor.

Below: Jordanian cooking includes many colorful and delicious dishes, such as these tasty appetizers.

Jordan's national dish is *mansaf* (MAN-saf), a Bedouin specialty that consists of seasoned chunks of lamb cooked in a yogurt-based sauce. It is served over rice. *Khubez* (KHO-biz), a type of bread, is eaten with every meal. It is usually round and flat and can come in many flavors and textures. Appetizers are also popular and include dishes such as *baba ghanoush* (BAH-ba GAH-nooj), a dip made of eggplant, and hummus, a paste made from chickpeas. Coffee is Jordan's most popular drink. It is often flavored with cardamom, a type of spice.

JORDAN

A B C D

1

2

3

4

5

LEBANON

SYRIA

IRAQ

MEDITERRANEAN SEA

Jordan

Syrian Desert

N

IRBID
● Irbid

'AJLOUN

JERASH
● Jerash

Uplands

MAFRAQ

WEST
BANK

BALQA'

■ AMMAN
Mount Nebo
(2,631 feet / 802 m)
▲
● Madaba

Al Azraq Oasis

MADABA

AMMAN

ZARQA

Jordan Valley

Dead
Sea

KARAK

ISRAEL

SAUDI

TAFILEH

ARABIA

● Shobak

MA'AN

GREAT RIFT VALLEY

Petra

AQABA

▲ Jabal Ram
(5,689 feet / 1,734 m)

Wadi
Rum

● Aqaba

Gulf of
Aqaba

——————	Country Boundary
————	Governorate Boundary
– – – –	Disputed Boundary
■	Capital
●	City
⋮	Historical Site
∼∼∼	River

Above: Spa resorts such as Wadi Zarga Ma'in in western Jordan attract many tourists.

'Ajloun (governorate) B2

Amman (city) B2

Amman (governorate) B2–C3

Aqaba A5

Aqaba (governorate) A4–B5

Balqa' (governorate) A2–B3

Dead Sea A3

Great Rift Valley A4–A5

Gulf of Aqaba A5

Iraq D1–D2

Irbid (city) B2

Irbid (governorate) A2–B2

Israel A1–A5

Jabal Ram A4

Jerash (city) B2

Jerash (governorate) B2

Jordan River B1–A3

Jordan Valley A3

Karak (governorate) A3–B3

Lebanon A1–B1

Ma'an (governorate) A4–C4

Madaba (city) B3

Madaba (governorate) A3–B3

Mafraq (governorate) B2–D3

Mediterranean Sea A1–A3

Mount Nebo B3

Petra A4

Saudi Arabia A5–D5

Shobak A4

Syria B1–D1

Tafileh (governorate) A3–B4

Wadi Rum A5

West Bank A2–A3

Zarqa (governorate) B2–C3

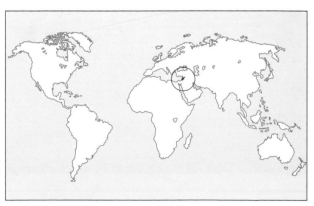

Glossary

annexed: took control of a piece of land or a country. Land that is annexed becomes part of another country.

apprentices: students who learn a trade by doing a job under the guidance of a skilled worker.

conquered: invaded and took over a land using violent force.

constitutional monarchy: a type of government that is led by a king or a queen but is ruled according to the laws of an established constitution.

dynasties: series of rulers, one after another, from the same family.

elevation: the height, or altitude, of a place above sea level.

empire: a very large collection of lands or regions ruled by one group.

ethnic: related to a race or a culture that has similar customs and languages.

export: a product sent out of a country to be sold in another country.

governorates: regions in a nation that have their own governing officials.

heritage: culture and traditions passed down by earlier generations.

imports: goods bought and shipped into a country from other countries.

inheritance: the act of receiving land or valuables after a family member dies.

mezzanine: a balcony with a low ceiling, usually built above the ground floor.

minerals: substances from the ground that are not made of animals or plants, such as rocks, salts, or phosphates.

mosaics: designs made of small tiles, usually set into a wall or floor.

nomadic: moving from place to place without having a permanent home.

phosphates: acids that can be used in items such as drinks or fertilizers.

pilgrimage: a journey made to a holy place as an act of religious devotion.

refugees: people who flee to another country to escape danger.

reserves: land set aside so that animals and plants can survive there.

revolt: a fight by citizens against the government, often involving violence.

sacrifices: personal needs and interests given up so others can have what they need and want.

stable: firm or steady; calm.

vocational: related to an occupation, profession, or skilled trade.

More Books to Read

The Arabs in the Golden Age. Peoples of the Past series. Mokhtar Moktefi (Millbrook Press)

The Dead Sea: The Saltiest Sea. Great Record Breakers in Nature series. Aileen Weintraub (Powerkids Press)

Jordan. Modern Nations of the World series. Karen Wills (Lucent Books)

The Middle East in Search of Peace. Cathryn J. Long (Millbrook Press)

Muslim Holidays. Faith Winchester (Bridgestone Books)

Muslim Mosque. Angela Wood (Gareth Stevens)

Saladin: Noble Prince of Islam. Diane Stanley (HarperCollins Juvenile Books)

Videos

Alif is for Asad!: Discover the Arabic Alphabet. (Library Video)

Jordan: Kingdom of the Desert. Geographical Odysseys series. (Choices, Inc.)

My Family From Jordan. (Schlessinger Media)

Ramadan. (Schlessinger Media)

Web Sites

cyberschoolbus.un.org/infonation/ index.asp?id=400

www.acsamman.edu.jo/~el/2/abc/

www.scc-jordan.com/photo.html

www.worldatlas.com/webimage/ countrys/asia/jo.htm

Due to the dynamic nature of the Internet, some web sites stay current longer than others. To find additional web sites, use a reliable search engine with one or more of the following keywords to help you locate information about Jordan. Keywords: *Amman, Aqaba, Bedouin, Dead Sea, Hashemite, Jerash, King Hussein, Syrian Desert.*

Index